THE COMPLETE HISTORY OF COMEDY (abridged)

Reed Martin

&

Austin Tichenor

BROADWAY PLAY PUBLISHING INC
New York
www.broadwayplaypub.com
info@broadwayplaypub.com

Cover art by Lar DeSouza. Used by permission.

First edition: February 2018
I S B N: 978-0-88145-744-5

Book design: Marie Donovan
Page make-up: Adobe InDesign
Typeface: Palatino

"Critic's Pick! Fast and furious...fresh and funny...a great piece of political satire."
Cincinnati City Beat

"The trio delivers 100 minutes filled with laughter to a delighted audience."
British Theatre Guide

"I don't want to get too philosophical here. Just know that you'll laugh. Not at everything, mind you. Some of the material may make you uncomfortable. It's supposed to. Mostly, though, you will laugh. Really hard. And smile so hard that—yes, it's a cliché, but it's true—your cheeks will hurt. When was the last time you went to the theater and had that sensation?"
Cincinnati Enquirer

"Very funny!"
Reviews Hub UK

"Easily one of the troupe's funniest, most inspired shows in years!"
Pacific Sun

"Wildly funny!"
LA Post Examiner

"It's a show about wit. About quick minds. About what makes us laugh. And what's fair game for laughter."
Cincinnati Enquirer

"Spectacular! (A) terrific rapid-fire, laugh-out-loud performance! A laugh-riot!"
Nashua Telegraph

"These guys are truly adept jokesters, physical shtick, wordplay, music, improv—they can do it all."
Cincinnati City Beat

"A non-stop, two-hour laugh fest!"
Lowell Sun

"A wild, wild ride! It's funny. Really, really funny… And most of all, it's really, really smart."
Cincinnati Enquirer

"You knew they'd get this one right. THE COMPLETE HISTORY OF COMEDY (abridged) is a madcap, breakneck-speed two hours. Audacious, often outrageous and bawdy, the frantic pacing of COMEDY reminds you of an old-time burlesque or vaudeville revue."
Boston Stages

"A dizzying night's entertainment…the work of some serious minds exploring the art of comedy."
Cincinnati City Beat

"My cheeks still hurt from laughing so much. Way too funny."
Napa Valley Register

"Exhaustingly hilarious. And the scope of their humor knows no bounds."
Cincinnati Enquirer

"THE COMPLETE HISTORY OF COMEDY (abridged) is a master class in the art form."
Broadway World

"Wonderful, whimsical. The wit, verve and creativity they manage to squeeze into (the show) are a winning formula that is anything but formulaic."
Fairfield Daily Republic

THE COMPLETE HISTORY OF COMEDY (abridged) was first presented as a workshop production by Napa Valley Playhouse in Napa, California from 30 August–15 September 2013. The cast and creative contributors were:

Cast	Dodds Delzell, Dan Saski, Chad Yarish
Directors	Reed Martin & Austin Tichenor
Stage manager	Jennifer Ruygt
Costume design	Skipper Skeoch
Sound design	Joe Winkler
Scenic design	Tim Hostslag & Bill Kaufman
Props	Alli Bostedt, Tim Holtslag, Michael Ross, Chad Yarish
Lighting design	April George
Puppets	Barbara McFadden
Slides	Barry Martin, Julie & Morgan McClelland, Annie Ruygt, Jenn Ruygt
Music	Peter Bufano
Crew	April George, Travis Brown

The world premiere production of THE COMPLETE HISTORY OF COMEDY (abridged) was performed by the Reduced Shakespeare Company at the Cincinnati Playhouse in the Park (Blake Robison, Artistic Director; Buzz Ward, Managing Director) from 9 November–29 December 2013. The play then had its European premiere at the Pleasance Courtyard in Edinburgh from 31 July–25 August 2014. The cast and creative contributors were:

Cast	Dominic Conti, Reed Martin, Austin Tichenor
Stage managers	Alli Bostedt, Jennifer Morrow, Davey Naylor
Set design	Phil Rundle
Lighting design	Catherin Girard
Costumes	Skipper Skeoch
Puppets: Supremes	Barbara McFadden
Dummy	Alli Bostedt, Ingrid Heithaus
Slides	Barry Martin, Julie & Morgan McClelland, Annie Ruygt, Jenn Ruygt
Music	Peter Bufano
Props	Alli Bostedt, Tim Holtslag, Michael Ross, Chad Yarish
Sound	Zach Moore, Joe Winkler
Timeline	Phil Rundle
Crew	Debra Hildebrand, Cian Martin, Lara Sheridan
R S C General Manager	Jane Martin
R S C Company Manager	Alli Bostedt

For their contributions to the development of the script, the authors wish to thank:

Dominic Conti; Alli Bostedt; Elaine Randolph; Dustin Sullivan; Jennifer King; Michael Ross and Napa Valley Playhouse; Blake Robison, Michael Haney and Buzz Ward at Cincinnati Playhouse in the Park; Charles Towers at Merrimack Repertory Theatre; Alan Ernstein; David Carlyon; Dee Ryan; Damian Cruden; Russ Lees; Daisy Tichenor; Bernard Levin; Quincy Tichenor; Campbell and Cian Martin; Jane Martin; Gary Rudoren; Peter Marks; Sonoma Valley High School Drama Department; Roger Rhoten of Sebastiani Theatre; Anthony Clarvoe; Vanessa Lee; and Dodds Delzell, Dan Saski, Jennifer Rugyt, Travis Brown and Chad Yarish. No sheep were harmed in the making of this stage play.

IMPORTANT NOTE

The use of the name
REDUCED SHAKESPEARE COMPANY
in any way whatsoever to publicize, promote, or
advertise any performance of this script
IS EXPRESSLY PROHIBITED

Likewise, any use of the name
REDUCED SHAKESPEARE COMPANY
within the actual live performance of this script
IS ALSO EXPRESSLY PROHIBITED.

The play must be billed as follows:

THE COMPLETE HISTORY OF COMEDY (abridged)
by
Reed Martin & Austin Tichenor

FOR WHAT IT'S WORTH

This published edition uses the names of the actors
from the original production, but we encourage
you to use the first and last names of your actual
actors. Similarly, you should use their actual physical
characteristics when the script calls for them.

We also encourage you to read the stage directions,
which have been written by the playwrights to describe
the business and physical moments used (successfully)
in the original production. We also encourage you to
ignore the stage directions if you want, but at least read
them. They'll definitely give you clues about what's
going on.

There are several topical references in the script, the
humor and relevance of which will fade over time.
Permission is granted to update those references. This
is not to say scenes should be rewritten (which is, in
fact, strictly prohibited) but rather we're giving you
permission to change a punch line or reference from
"Adam Sandler" to…honestly, is anybody going to
come along as unfunny as Adam Sandler? We think
not.

In our experience, the script works best when it's
performed simply, seriously, and passionately. That is
to say, the script is funny so play it straight. It seems
obvious but it bears repeating: these three characters
are trying to do nothing less than save the world—

and they only have two hours to do it. Their intensity gives the show energy and pace, and the comic conflict comes from their differing opinions and approaches. If your production's running longer than about an hour and forty-five minutes (including intermission), you're doing it wrong.

ACT ONE

(The set consists of one 8' by 8' seamed drop or panel that looks solid enough from the front, but is actually made of two pieces of stretchy fabric that meet in the middle and allow people or props to pass through a center seam. It's surrounded by black curtains. Actors enter from either side of it.)

(A caveman [AUSTIN] and cavewoman [DOM] enter. She is heavily pregnant. As they cross, she goes into labor and, squatting, delivers a beautiful cavebaby doll. The cavewoman has more contractions and delivers a second cavebaby. She then delivers ten more babies in quick succession. All these births can be achieved by having the cavewoman stand in the up center entrance or doorway and having someone throw baby dolls onstage through the cavewoman's legs. The caveman picks up and carries the dolls off as the cavewoman collapses in exhaustion.)

(Now she goes into more labor and delivers a live, full-sized baby [REED] who sucks on a pacifier as he crawls between her legs while she stands in the doorway. The caveman returns smoking a cigar, startling the baby who quickly crawls back in the womb. The cavewoman orders the caveman to give chase, which he does by climbing inside. The cavewoman makes movements like there's a chase going on inside her. The caveman emerges with the rattle but no baby. Then the baby emerges smoking a cigar. They all hug, one happy family.)

(Blackout. Lights up on AUSTIN.*)*

AUSTIN: And that, ladies and gentlemen, was the birth of Comedy. How do we know? Because we have discovered the single most important artifact in the history of mankind. Good evening, I'm Austin Tichenor.

*(*REED *and* DOM *enter, all business.)*

DOM: I'm Dominic Conti.

REED: I'm Reed Martin. *(Exiting)* Excuse me.

AUSTIN: Yes, thank you, Reed.

DOM: Austin and I made this incredible discovery while visiting the San Francisco Public Library.

(Latecomers should be seated here, if necessary. The guys can abuse them if desired, then continue. Best to make it look like you'd like to continue with the show, but the interruption can't be ignored and the show's stopped anyway, so you might as well find out what the hold up was and why the audience members were late.)

AUSTIN: That's right. Dom and I were making our annual pilgrimage to the Schmulowitz Collection of Wit and Humor.

DOM: It was there that a man in a black bowler hat directed us toward a small, dusty trunk hidden in the corner. Then he opened the trunk, revealing a large fortune cookie which he then cracked open. And what was inside? A fortune.

AUSTIN: Many of you are probably familiar with *The Art of War*, the definitive work on military strategy and tactics written two thousand years ago by Chinese general Sun-Tzu. Well, ladies and gentlemen, this is *The Art of Comedy*.

(Reverential music. REED *enters wearing white gloves and carefully carrying an ancient manuscript.)*

DOM: Thank you, Reed. Now, *The Art of Comedy* was written by Sun-Tzu's younger brother, who lived long ago in the Longdong Province during the Wang Dynasty.

AUSTIN: Scholars believed no copy of *The Art of Comedy* had survived.

DOM: *The Art of Comedy* was so popular and so influential that Sun-Tzu killed his brother in a fit of jealous rage and destroyed all copies of the book. All copies—save one.

AUSTIN: The man in the black bowler hat said because these comic teachings have been lost for two thousand years, the world is spiraling into a state of unhappiness and war.

DOM: He said he had a mission for us.

AUSTIN: He said it's imperative we share this book with the entire world.

DOM: He said if we don't, this unrest will become irreversible.

AUSTIN: He said we must also tell the story of all the comic artistry that came after this book was written.

DOM: He said—well, he wouldn't shut up, frankly.

REED: I'm glad I wasn't there.

DOM: And then like that…

(They all blow through their hands.)

DOM: …he was gone.

AUSTIN: So tonight our mission is clear: Save the world through the art of Comedy.

DOM: But what my esteemed and semi-oblivious colleague is neglecting to tell you is that we face a tremendous obstacle. Show them, Reed.

(REED *opens the book to reveal a spot near the back of the book where a number of pages have been torn out.*)

DOM: You're opening it backwards.

AUSTIN: No, the Chinese read back to front.

DOM: Oh, right. We can't share the entirety of this book with the world because the thirteenth and final chapter is missing.

AUSTIN: Details. *(Pulling out a spiral notebook with handwritten text in it)* Because the *The Art of Comedy* is in Chinese I have translated the first twelve chapters we *do* have into English.

DOM: And although we don't know how it's going to finish, tonight we will share with you the wisdom of *The Art of Comedy* through everything that has come after.

AUSTIN: But—and I have a very big but—because we're telling the history of comedy in all of its forms, we will also be covering the humor of bodily functions. We will be discussing farts. We will make fun of bottoms, we will embrace comically large bosoms, and we will touch upon penises of all sizes. Also, I must warn you that tonight we will use the occasional swear word. These are fine Anglo-Saxon words which I'm sure none of you have ever heard before, but if there are any children in the audience tonight, please: Cover your parents' ears. They'll be embarrassed by what you're hearing but don't worry: this is just a phase and as you get older, they'll grow out of it. Gentlemen?

(AUSTIN *hands* REED *his translation.* REED *very carefully hands the ancient manuscript to* AUSTIN.)

ALL: *(With ritual seriousness)* W-W-R-D.

(AUSTIN *and* DOM *start to go but* AUSTIN *stops.*)

AUSTIN: Oh, and one final warning: Before the night is over, we are going to hit someone in this theatre in the face with a pie. Enjoy the show!

(AUSTIN and DOM exit.)

REED: Chapter One of *The Art of Comedy*. *(Reading)* "Why did the chicken cross the road?" Anyone?

(The audience answers, "To get to the other side".)

REED: Exactly right. *The Art of Comedy* begins with this classic. So we begin our journey through the history of comedy by demonstrating how this single joke has evolved over time. The cavemen told it like this.

(AUSTIN and DOM enter as cavemen.)

DOM: Why chicken cross road?

(AUSTIN hits DOM over the head with a club and exits. DOM exits, laughing. That's the funniest punch line ever.)

REED: Thousands of years later, with the dawn of Western Civilization, theatre was invented and the ancient Greeks told the joke like this.

(AUSTIN and DOM wear white sheets and Greek style masks. They use ritualistic gestures, perfectly in unison.)

AUSTIN/DOM: Oh, brave Clytemnestra! The chicken has fallen victim to the sins of the father rooster. The hens have come home to roost. As his father before him, the brave chicken has tragically followed a path over which he has no control and now lies flattened against the stones. *(They exit.)*

REED: Hundreds of years passed and in Elizabethan England at the Globe Theatre in London, William Shakespeare put it this way.

AUSTIN: *(In a hint of Shakespearean garb)* To cross or not to cross? That is the question. Whether 'tis nobler for the hen to suffer the slings and arrows of oncoming traffic or to take wing above a sea of commuters and by o'erflying, avoid them? Or void o'er them? *(He exits.)*

REED: And then, there was Burlesque.

DOM: *(With hat and bike horn)* Hey hey! Why did the chicken cross the road? She was looking for a pecker. *(He honks his horn and then opens his coat, revealing a rubber chicken sticking up from the waist of his trousers. Pulling the rubber chicken out of his pants)* Whoah! How'd that get down there? I think she wanted a little cock in her doodle-doo, you know what I mean? *(Honks bike horn and exits)*

REED: Soon there was post-modernism.

(AUSTIN and DOM enter wearing battered bowler hats.)

DOM: Let's cross the road.

AUSTIN: Yes, let's.

DOM: But we can't.

AUSTIN: Why not?

DOM: We're waiting for the chicken.

(AUSTIN and DOM exit.)

REED: And in Paris, as always, they insisted on telling the joke in what they considered a uniquely French way.

(DOM, as Marcel Marceau, tells the joke in mime—finishing by waving a small white flag and exiting.)

REED: And of course the British did it this way.

(AUSTIN enters in drag with comically large bosoms.)

AUSTIN: *(In Monty Python accent)* Why did the chicken cross the road? Who cares? I'm dressed like a lady! Ha, ha, ha! *(He exits.)*

REED: And we would be remiss in our examination of the history of this joke if we neglected to include the Japanese game show.

(DOM *enters dressed in bowl cut wig and Sumo loin cloth. He bows. He speaks in pigeon Japanese and holds a prop chicken.)*

DOM: Hyiiiaaaahhhh. Orokana niwatori! (*"Foolish chicken." Pointing to chicken)* A bok bok. (*He bows and moves the chicken around as if it's walking. Then he places the chicken behind the center masking and reveals a large mallet.)* Hiiiiii!

(DOM *"smashes" the chicken and* AUSTIN *throws feathers out the other side of the center masking.* DOM *bows and exits.)*

REED: But the Chicken Crossing the Road reached its cultural apex in the middle of the twentieth century in New York City with the advent of the big Broadway musical!

(AUSTIN *and* DOM *enter as chickens, wearing coxcombs and sleeves with yellow feathers. They do a chorus kick-line and sing up tempo.)*

AUSTIN/DOM: Yada-da-da-da-da! (*Singing à la* There's No Business Like Show Business)
There's no crossing
Like our crossing
And we'll cross if we can
We must be brave 'cause this is not the time to cry
We'll walk across because we can't fly
We might get flattened but we simply have to try
Or we'll fry in a pan!

(AUSTIN *and* DOM *exit to applause. As* REED *talks, he pulls a projection screen down [or on] or moves to next to it where it lives onstage.)*

REED: Chapter 2 of *The Art of Comedy*— "To learn what is funny, study what is not funny." And as I've always said, a picture is worth a thousand words. So now, ladies and gentlemen, here are the Top Six Least Funny People of All Time— *(Checking his pockets for the projector remote control)* Dom!

(DOM runs on.)

DOM: Yeah?

REED: Have you seen my clicker?

DOM: *(Checking his pockets)* I don't—oh, here it is!

REED: I thought so.

DOM: Well, I'm glad we found it. *(He starts to exit.)*

REED: Dom!

DOM: Oh. Right.

(DOM gives REED the clicker and exits.)

REED: Thank you. Sorry about that. And now ladies and gentlemen, here they are, the Top Six Least Funny People of All Time.

(REED clicks through a series of pictures that appear onscreen.)

REED: Number 6—

(Clicks; a picture of Attila the Hun appears on the screen.)

REED: Attila the Hun. Great at pillaging. Not great at parties. Number 5—

(Clicks; picture of Rasputin appears.)

REED: Rasputin. Funny odd, yes. Funny ha ha, no. The Number 4 Least Funny People Of All Time—

(Clicks; classic image of a rotund opera singer wearing a horned helmet appears.)

REED: Germans. Number 3—

(Clicks; new picture)

REED: Adam Sandler. Number 2—

(Clicks; new picture: somebody horrible in the news. Past people have included Anthony Weiner and Kim Davis.)

REED: And the Number One least funny people of all time—

(Clicks; a picture of a mime appears.)

REED: —Mimes!

(DOM enters in a striped shirt and black beret. He's angry at REED for putting mimes on the list.)

REED: Uh-oh. Dom disagrees with me about mimes. He thinks I'm crazy.

(DOM mimes "crazy".)

REED: *(To the audience)* Dom loves mimes.

(DOM makes hand over heart gesture, then mimes Munch's The Scream *with his hands over his ears.)*

REED: He feels that the world is too noisy a place.

(DOM mimes listening.)

REED: He loves the silence of the mimes.

(DOM does a rope pull.)

REED: He is adept at the rope pull…

(DOM walks in place.)

REED: …at walking…

(DOM attempts to "Walk Against the Wind".)

REED: As you can see, he's terrible at walking against the wind.

(DOM gives REED the "Up Yours" gesture.)

REED: Sorry. *(To audience)* Mimes don't like to be mocked.

(DOM *does "tsk tsk" fingers to* REED, *then continues with a series of mime moves, at first relating to what* REED *is talking about and quickly growing more and more outrageous and left field.)*

REED: They believe mime is an effective way to express complex thoughts and ideas. In fact, mime is such an effective means of communication that I'm standing here having to explain the meaning of every single thing Dom is trying to convey.

DOM: All right, stop it!

REED: Sh! Mimes don't talk.

DOM: They can. Unfortunately everyone associates mimes with mute dumb-asses in berets!

(DOM *grabs the clicker and makes the mime image disappear, then pockets the clicker. He begins to build a mimed box around* REED, *using a pantomime drill to drive in imaginary screws.)*

DOM: Nobody gets this!

REED: What?

DOM: Yes, before there was language, the very first performers were mimes.

REED: Great! How about—

DOM: *(Going right on)* But mime does not mean mute! The original definition is "to imitate both physically and vocally"!

REED: That's very interesting—

DOM: *(Going right on)* Mimes only became silent when the censors in England outlawed plays with dialogue.

REED: Could you wrap this—

DOM: *(Going right on)* So there is no reason that mimes can't make noise.

REED: Come on, Dom. These boxes never—

(DOM *closes a mime window in front of* REED's *face.* REED *keeps moving his lips, but no longer makes any sound.*)

DOM: We talk. We squawk. Get used to it.

(DOM *exits.* REED *is "trapped" in the box, pounding on the "wall" with his hands. Silently he mouths, "Help! Help me!". Blackout*)

(*Lights up on* AUSTIN *holding his translation of* The Art of Comedy *in the spiral notebook.*)

AUSTIN: Chapter Three of *The Art of Comedy*— "Comic Vocabulary."

(REED *and* DOM *demonstrate what* AUSTIN *describes.*)

AUSTIN: The Take.

(REED *and* DOM *take in unison.*)

AUSTIN: The Slow Burn.

(REED *and* DOM *demonstrate in unison.*)

AUSTIN: The Double Take.

(REED *and* DOM *double take in unison.*)

AUSTIN: The Raspberry.

(*In unison* REED *and* DOM *stick their tongues out and blow them.*)

AUSTIN: The Double Take Slow Burn—

(REED *and* DOM *demonstrate…*)

AUSTIN: —with a Homer Simpson.

REED/DOM: D'oh!

AUSTIN: The Trip.

(REED *trips* DOM.)

AUSTIN: The Trip.

(DOM *trips again.*)

AUSTIN: The Rule of Threes.

(DOM *steps nimbly over* REED's *foot and then trips on his own and falls hard to the floor.* REED *laughs.* DOM, *angry, gets up and slaps* REED. AUSTIN *is pleasantly surprised.*)

AUSTIN: Oh, the Slap!

(REED *retaliates by back-handing Dom.*)

AUSTIN: The Backhand.

(DOM *punches* REED.)

AUSTIN: The Straight Punch.

(REED *punches* DOM *like a speed bag.*)

AUSTIN: The Rolling Punch.

(REED *punches Dom with a right cross.*)

AUSTIN: With a Cross!

(DOM *spins and falls to the floor*)

AUSTIN: And a corkscrew. Oh, and here comes the Hair Pull!

(REED *grabs* DOM *by the hair and starts to pull him offstage.*)

DOM: Ow ow ow! Okay, wait. We've got to stop this.

REED: Why?

(REED *slams* DOM's *head to the ground.*)

DOM: There are children watching!

AUSTIN: So?

DOM: So they'll see this behavior and try to imitate it.

AUSTIN: Kids don't do that! *(He exits.)*

DOM: My brother did. We watched the Three Stooges then he beat the crap out of me.

REED: Oh grow up. Nothing is more American than Slapstick. It's practically guaranteed in the Second Amendment.

DOM: What about wit? What about style?

(AUSTIN *enters carrying two pies.* [*Disposable aluminum pie tins filled with shaving cream are easy to wash out of clothing and don't leave a sour smell over time as real cream does.*])

AUSTIN: What about pies?

DOM: Woah! Put those away.

AUSTIN: Why?

DOM: We need to talk about pie control.

REED: (*Taking a pie from* AUSTIN) No we don't. We need to enforce existing pie laws! Pies aren't the problem!

AUSTIN: You'll get my pie when you pry it from my cold cream-covered fingers.

REED: Pies don't pie people—

REED/AUSTIN: People pie people.

DOM: (*Running off*) Aah!

AUSTIN: (*Giving the pies to* REED) Liberals. Here, lock these up. We don't want them to go off. Yet.

(REED *exits*)

AUSTIN: Anyway, Chapter Four of *The Art of Comedy* is called "Fear Of The Other". So who here's racist, anybody? Well, you're in the right place. It seems that ethnic and national stereotypes go back to the very beginning.

(AUSTIN *exits.* REED *enters holding a parchment or animal skin with a map of the world on it.*)

REED: Okay, listen up everybody. Most of you know me, I'm Sam the Caveman.

AUSTIN/DOM: (*Off stage*) Hi, Sam.

REED: The good news is, we're not swinging from trees anymore, and we're not Neanderthals running around grunting and throwing our crap at each other—except for you, Phil. Knock it off. The time has come to spread out and settle this big rock we're on. So I want each of you to come up here. We'll decide what tribe you're gonna be and where you should live.

(DOM *enters, walking stiffly. He speaks without an accent.*)

REED: Name?

DOM: Nigel.

REED: Something wrong with your upper lip?

DOM: It's stiff.

REED: You walking funny?

DOM: I have a stick up my ass.

REED: Nigel, you're going to England!

DOM: Jolly good!

(DOM *leaves.* AUSTIN *comes in, using an exaggerated Italian accent and using his hands a lot.*)

AUSTIN: Hey! Whassamatta for you, ah?

REED: Name?

AUSTIN: I'm-a Tony! My wife, she's-a gotta the big-a bazooms, I make-a the pasta, and I keep everything-a organized: my sauces, my Chianti, and my crime.

REED: Tony. You're going to New Jersey.

AUSTIN: Grazie! (*He exits.*)

REED: Next!

(DOM *enters wearing a striped prisoner's shirt and cap.*)

REED: Australia! Next!

(DOM *exits as* AUSTIN *enters wearing a huge Afro. He speaks impeccably.*)

REED: Name?

AUSTIN: Kevin.

REED: Really?

AUSTIN: What, you don't like Kevin?

REED: No, it's fine. It just feels like it needs some extra consonants and a weird pronunciation.

AUSTIN: How about Quayvonn? With a Q.

REED: Perfect. Quayvonn, you're going to Africa!

AUSTIN: Aw, I wanted to go to America!

REED: *(Cheerfully)* We'll send ships to bring you over later.

AUSTIN: Solid.

*(*REED *tries to high five, but* AUSTIN *just looks at him.)*

AUSTIN: *(Exiting)* Aw, Neanderthal, please.

*(*DOM *enters, wildly intoxicated.)*

DOM: Top o' the mornin' to ya!

REED: *(Without looking up)* Boston! Next!

*(*DOM *lurches off.* AUSTIN *enters.)*

REED: Name?

*(*AUSTIN *looks confused.)*

*(*REED *says the name of a town or state nearby that everyone makes fun of.)*

(As AUSTIN *exits:)*

REED: Next! Oh, that's me. Since I think I know what's best for everyone else in the world, I'll go to America!

(Blackout. REED *exits.* AUSTIN *enters holding the traditional masks of Comedy and Tragedy. If there are more latecomers, bring them in here.)*

AUSTIN: *(Holding them up)* These are the death masks of Sun-Tzu and his younger brother Ah-Tzu. See how happy Ah-Tzu was? La-la-la! Comedy is funny! And see how angry and jealous and bitter and homicidal

Sun-Tzu was? Grr. I'm gonna kill you and take your book! Arr. Of course now these masks have come to represent Tragedy and the greatest of all theatrical arts, Comedy.

(DOM *enters holding the spiral notebook translation.*)

DOM: I'm surprised you don't think Tragedy is the greatest theatrical art form.

AUSTIN: Well, if by greatest you mean most overrated, then yes, I do.

DOM: What?

AUSTIN: Absolutely. Anybody can make an audience sit quietly. *(Beat)* We're doing it right now. You know, one of the answers to the question "WWRD?" is, preach the Gospel. Comedy does not get the respect it deserves.

DOM: Well, Ah-Tzu agrees with you. *(Reading)* Chapter Five: "Study the Comic Masters."

AUSTIN: Yes, like the Catholic Church.

DOM: What?

AUSTIN: Absolutely. I know it sounds weird, but one of the very first joke books ever written was called *Liber Facetiarum*, published in Italy in 1451. The jokes were gathered from an actual organization called the Vatican Joke Club.

DOM: *(Exiting)* Yes! Enlightening and spiritual!

AUSTIN: *(Exiting)* No! Dirty and blasphemous!

(Light change. Three 15th century clergymen enter, wearing brown monk robes. They sing solemnly.)

ALL: Did you hear that Father Glass
Refuses to serve Sunday Mass
He risks eternity in Hell
So he can watch the N F L
(Sung like "amen") Ha, ha

(For a recording of this melody, please go to BroadwayPlayPub.com)

REED: In the name of the knock knock, the riddle, and the double entrendre—

ALL: *(Said like "amen")* Ha, ha.

REED: Let us begin by acknowledging our faults and so prepare us for the sacred hilarities.

ALL: I confess that I have greatly punned, in my thoughts and in my words, in jokes I have said and in jokes I have failed to say, *(Striking their breast)* through my schmaltz, through my schmaltz, through my most grievous schmaltz; therefore I ask the blessed Virgin Mary, And all the Stand ups and Clowns, and you, my brothers and sisters—well, actually just brothers—to pray for me to the Lord our God. May he spray seltzer on us, forgive us our puns, and bring us to everlasting laughs. *(Said like "Amen")* Ha ha.

REED: *(Opening a small book)* Our first reading today comes from the book of Hypocrites, Chapter 2, verses 1 through 6. *(Reading)* A nun at a Catholic school asked her students what they wanted to be when they grew up. Little Susie declared, "I want to be a prostitute." "What did you say?" asked the nun, completely shocked. "I said I want to be a prostitute." "Oh, thank goodness," said the nun. "I thought you said you wanted to be a Protestant!" *(À la "The word of God")* The word of Guffawed.

ALL: *(Said like "Amen")* Ha, ha.

DOM: Our second reading today is from the book of Libidinous. *(Reading)* An old man bursts into the confessional and says to the priest, "I've got to tell you this. For the thirty years I've been married to my wife I've never cheated. Then this beautiful young woman moved in next door and since then we've been fornicating like crazy!" And the priest says, "How long has it been since your last Confession?" And the man says, "I've never been to Confession. I'm Jewish." "Then why are you telling me this?" And the man says, "Are you kidding? I'm telling everyone!" *(As before)* The word of Guffawed.

ALL: *(Said like "Amen")* Ha, ha.

AUSTIN: Our final reading comes from Second Comicals. *(Reading)* One day our Lord Jesus Christ did walk into a hotel, place three nails upon the counter, and ask, "Can you put me up for the night?"

(If the audience groans)

AUSTIN: And there was much groaning. *(As before)* The word of Guffawed.

ALL: *(Said like "Amen")* Ha, ha.

REED: Let us offer one another a sign of caprice.

(They turn to each other and do silly sounds and gestures.)

REED: A quick announcement before we conclude our meeting today. It seems that Sister Mary Louise managed to get herself pregnant at the Vatican Halloween Party.

DOM: *(Together with AUSTIN)* Well, she was hitting that sacramental wine.

AUSTIN: *(Together with DOM)* Who didn't see that coming…?

REED: Yes, I know. So next year please remind all the nuns not to dress up like altar boys.

(If the audience groans again)

REED: And there was even more groaning. Our morass is ended. Let us go in peace to love and unnerve the bored.

ALL: Ha ha. *(They sing again.)*
Hey hey we have got monk knees
We kneel upon them when we pray
And most of us have joined the Church
To hide the fact that we are gay
Black…out!

(The lights blackout as they sing "Out!".)

(Light up on DOM *wearing an Arlecchino suit, hat, mask and slapstick.)*

DOM: Buonasera! Il mio nome è Arlecchino. Commedia dell'Arte emerged during the Italian Renaissance as a form of physical theatre that involved broad comedy and highly structured improvisation. Scenes were connected by comic business or shtick called "lazzi" which literally means "To tie together." Performers were what we would call today "buskers" or street performers and were the first truly professional actors in history. Stock characters were identified by costumes, masks, and props. The most popular character was named Arlecchino, or the Harlequin, a merry trickster and servant to the upper class characters, whom he would often outwit. Arlecchino would often carry a slapstick— *(He demonstrates.)* — which, unfortunately, has become synonymous with stupid lowbrow comedy. Arlecchino was acrobatic— *(He does something physical: a fall or a high kick or a cartwheel.)* —hungry— *(He mimes catching a fly and eating it.)* —and horny. *(À la Borat to a woman in the audience)* Very nice. I like. *(As himself)* When he wasn't desperate for something to eat, he was trying to seduce the most beautiful woman in the audience. *(To a man)* You, sir. *(To a woman)* Pardon me. You, ma'am. Other popular characters included Capitano—

*(*REED *enters as* CAPITANO, *with mask and sword)*

DOM: The swaggering Spanish soldier who would exaggerate his conquests, both military and romantic.

(REED *freezes;* AUSTIN *enters, doddering.*)

DOM: And Dottore, the old pompous and fraudulent academic.

REED/CAPITANO: *(Singing)*
Oh Lady of *(Local city)*, I adore you...

AUSTIN/DOTTORE: Felicitas, est bonas, nice ass.

(DOM *quietly gives instructions to the woman as* CAPITANO *and* DOTTORE *speak.* CAPITANO *has a small bunch of flowers.* DOTTORE *has a box of candy.*)

REED/CAPITANO: I have conquered Aragon. I have conquered Portugal. And I will conquer her!

AUSTIN/DOTTORE: Nonsense, sir! Women prefer brains over brawn. Stand aside...

(*They approach the woman in the audience.* ARLECCHINO *rushes to intercept them.*)

DOM/ARLECCHINO: Gentlemen, gentlemen! One moment.

(DOM *whispers in* AUSTIN's *ear and takes his candy, then whispers in* REED's *ear and takes his flowers.*)

REED/CAPITANO: I have been deflowered! So that I may deflower her!

DOM/ARLECCHINO: I shall prepare her for you.

(DOM *goes back to the woman to coach her on what she's about to do.*)

AUSTIN/DOTTORE: Stand aside, sir. Age before stupidity!

REED/CAPITANO: Then you should-a go twice.

AUSTIN: *(To the woman in the audience)* My dear, I love you so much I won't give you any candy because you're already too fat!

(The woman [coached by DOM*] mime-slaps* AUSTIN*'s face while* DOM *slaps the slapstick to make the noise.* AUSTIN *screams and exits as* REED *approaches the woman.)*

REED/CAPITANO: Señorita, you are like a rose because your odor is so strong it attracts flies!

(Again, the woman slaps his face as DOM *makes the noise.)*

REED/CAPITANO: Pardonamé! *(To* DOM*)* My name is Inigo Capitano. You killed my romance. Prepare to die.

*(*DOM *slaps the slapstick again)*

REED/CAPITANO: Another day! *(He hurries off.)*

DOM/ARLECCHINO: To the most sweet, beautiful flower in the garden. *(Handing the flowers to the man)* You, sir! How about some applause for our wonderful volunteer?

(As they clap, he slides the flowers and candy off, then moves towards the screen.)

DOM: Now there were dozens of other colorful Commedia characters besides Arlecchino, Capitano and Dottore. They included Joe Torre...

(Click; slide of Joe Torre)

DOM: ...the greatest baseball manager of all time. There was also the old, greedy, cuckolded merchant called...

(Click; slide of Pantalone)

DOM: ...Pantalone, who always enjoyed a bowl of...

(Click; slide of minestrone soup)

DOM: ...Minestrone. Then there's the dwarfish, violent hunchback called...

(Click; slide of Pulcinella)

DOM: ...Pulcinella. And the Italian crime boss known as...

(Slick; slide of DeNiro, Pesci and Liotta)

DOM: ...A Gooda Fella. Arlecchino's comic sidekicks included the hot and spicy Jalapeño...

(Click; slide of a cartoon red pepper)

DOM: He also had an older sidekick known for over-acting called...

(Click; slide of Al Pacino)

DOM: ...Al Paciño. Hoo-ha! Then there was the grumpy bald character called—

(As Reed enters; surprised)

DOM: Reed!

REED: Hey, what are you doing with my pictures?

DOM: Your pictures? I thought they were everybody's pictures.

REED: No, I had them in an order.

DOM: Okay, okay. Relax. Here—

(DOM repeats the Commedia business by pretending the clicker is a fly buzzing around REED, then putting the clicker into his hand but pulling it away at the last second. They both have a good laugh at this. Then REED suddenly kicks DOM in the nuts.)

DOM: *(Doubled over, he hands REED the clicker and exits.)* What did you do that for?

REED: You'll see. Sorry about that. Now since we're examining the history of comedy, I thought we should take a look at the Top Eight Funniest People From The Olden Days. In order of funniness, Number 8—

(Click; a new picture)

REED: Molière. French playwright from the 1600s. The French consider him on a par with Shakespeare, but they think the same thing about Jerry Lewis. Number 7—

(Click; a new picture)

REED: Plautus. Most famous comedy writer from ancient Rome. The Number 6 funniest people from the olden days—

(Click; a new picture of many famous Jewish comics)

REED: Jews! Number 5—

(Click; a new picture)

REED: Joseph Grimaldi. Considered the father of modern clowns. Born London 1778. Credited with inventing the rubber chicken. Number 4—

(Click; a picture of Vlad the Impaler taking a hit of his asthma medicine)

REED: Vlad the Inhaler! Number 3—

(Click; a picture of Napoleon Dynamite dressed and posed like Napoleon Bonaparte)

REED: Napoleon. Number 2—

(Click; a new picture)

REED: Betty White! *(Or whoever is the oldest famous person that everyone is familiar with.)* And the number one funniest people from the olden days—

(Click; a photo-shopped picture of...)

REED: Mark and Shania Twain!

(REED clicks the picture off.)

REED: Thank you.

(REED exits. AUSTIN sneaks on, holding his notebook.)

AUSTIN: Now, in translating Chapter Six of *The Art of Comedy*, there were some Chinese slang words I didn't recognize at first. But it turns out that *see, liu, diu, hai, tsui siu, diu lay lo mo*, and *bo* are the words George Carlin translated into his Seven Dirty Words You Can't Say On Television. In English, they are— *(Ticking them off)* Shit, piss, fu…

DOM: *(Running on)* Whoa, Austin! Knock it off! This is not the place!

AUSTIN: Come on! The theater is the perfect place to discuss language.

DOM: We don't want to offend the good people of *(Name of town)*.

AUSTIN: They're just words.

DOM: Yes, words that represent something.

AUSTIN: Wait, it's what the words represent that would offend people?

DOM: Exactly.

AUSTIN: Why?

DOM: Religious reasons, for one.

AUSTIN: Well, those people can go forth and multiply themselves.

DOM: Austin! If you say the seven dirty words then the folks who run the theater are going to get letters and emails, and parents will have to explain it to their kids.

AUSTIN: That's a great conversation to have with kids, about words and their meanings and what is and isn't appropriate in what context.

DOM: Are you crazy? Parents don't want to talk to their kids!

AUSTIN: *You're* crazy! These words have been said in this theater hundreds of times!

DOM: Yes, but I don't use those words, and people don't expect that kind of language from us. You'd expect it in a show by David Mamet.

AUSTIN: That doesn't mean we can't—

DOM: *(Cutting him off)* Oh—! That reminds me of a theater joke. There's a homeless man outside a theater and he wants to borrow a dollar from this guy. The guy says "In the words of William Shakespeare, neither a borrower nor a lender be." And the homeless man says, "In the words of David Mamet, fuck you."

AUSTIN: Ah-ha!

(Blackout)

DOM: *(In the burn)* Shit.

(Lights up on REED.)

REED: Chapter Seven. "Critics say the darnedest things."

(Lights up on AUSTIN, holding a newspaper clipping.)

AUSTIN: *(Reading)* "Monty Python's Dead Parrot Sketch is a comic disaster. No pet shop owner would actually sell someone a dead parrot and then claim it was still alive. While Mr Cleese and Mr Palin are clearly talented and likeable performers, they are saddled with sub-par material."

(AUSTIN exits. Lights up on REED, holding a newspaper clipping.)

REED: *(Reading)* "If Mel Brooks thinks that a musical called *Springtime for Hitler* is going to tickle funny bones, then sadly he is in for a rude awakening. The audience should be ashamed of itself for the standing ovation it gave this outrage of a show."

(REED exits. Lights up on DOM, holding a newspaper clipping.)

DOM: *(Reading)* "It gives this critic no pleasure to report that the recent comedy sketch by Abbott and Costello is doomed by its weak premise. Nobody has the surnames Who, What, or I Don't Know. Why the audience was rolling in the aisles is beyond me. It's certainly no Shakespeare."

(DOM exits. AUSTIN enters wearing Elizabethan garb.)

AUSTIN/COSTELLO: Ah, what a glorious day it is here in the Elizabethan Era! A perfect day to attend the theatre, and with so many playhouses to choose from! *(Pointing to each)* The Rose, The Curtain, the Theatre—

(REED enters, dressed similarly.)

REED/ABBOTT: Oh, Petruchio Costello!

AUSTIN/COSTELLO: Ah, Friar Abbott!

REED/ABBOTT: Art thou bound for The Theater?

AUSTIN/COSTELLO: Aye, verily. I'm bound for The Rose.

REED/ABBOTT: So thou art not bound for The Theater?

AUSTIN/COSTELLO: Aye, my Lord. 'Tis The Rose for which I'm bound.

REED/ABBOTT: Good sir, I remain confused. Thou sayest thou art not bound for The Theater.

AUSTIN/COSTELLO: Sir, you remain witless and deaf. The theater is my destination. I'm bound for the Rose!

REED/ABBOTT: But not The Theater?

AUSTIN/COSTELLO: Aye, the theater, thou shit-headed Shakespearean! What strange malady possesseth thee? I'm going to the Rose Theater!

REED/ABBOTT: *(Realizing; laughing)* Ah, now I perceive that we might have been at cross-purposes. I ask if you're going to The Theater, Burbage's specifically-named playhouse.

AUSTIN/COSTELLO: *(Also laughing)* I mistook you, sir. I thought thou maintained some foul malevolence towards The Rose.

REED/ABBOTT: No, sir. The Rose, by any other name…

BOTH: *(Rapidly)* Blah blah blah blah blah blah blah blah blah.

AUSTIN/COSTELLO: I needs must be off, good Friar, or I shall miss the curtain.

REED/ABBOTT: *(Pointing)* My lord, the Curtain is that way.

AUSTIN/COSTELLO: Why do you tell me this?

REED/ABBOTT: I don't know.

BOTH: Third base! *(Bowing grandly)* Thank you very much.

(REED takes AUSTIN's Elizabethan garb and exits.)

AUSTIN: Now, that was obviously a homage to one of the funniest sketches ever written. So let me ask, does anyone know what is the funniest book ever written?

(AUSTIN either goes on, or if he gets an answer from someone, says)

AUSTIN: Excellent guess, but wrong. The funniest book ever written is *Jokes and Their Relation to the Unconscious* by Sigmund Freud. Seriously, pick it up. It's hysterical. Freud believed that jokes result from the conscious mind expressing forbidden thoughts. Emotions are bottled up and then released like gas venting to avoid an explosion.

(REED has entered upstage. He makes a fart sound.)

AUSTIN: Oh very funny.

(REED makes another fart noise.)

AUSTIN: Stop it!

(REED *does it again.*)

AUSTIN: Would you get out of here! Farts are just the lowest common denominator.

REED: Farts are funny! They're the original joke. And they smell so deaf people can enjoy them, too! And for your information Homer, Chaucer, and Mark Twain all wrote fart jokes.

AUSTIN: Yes, but they were masters. Farts should not be left in the hands of amateurs.

REED: Farts shouldn't be left in anyone's hands. And I'll tell you right now. Funny is funny. (*He makes very long and silly fart noise.*)

AUSTIN: Would you get out of here?!

(REED *exits.*)

AUSTIN: See, kids? Stay in school. Now, the second funniest thing ever written was Henri Bergson's essay from 1900 called *Laughter*. Bergson argued that comedy springs from the human body behaving like a machine. It's funny when a body is rigid.

(REED *has re-entered, carrying a mic on a stand.*)

REED: I know I smile when I'm rigid.

(AUSTIN *laughs genuinely and then says, equally genuinely:*)

AUSTIN: That's not funny.

REED: You laughed.

AUSTIN: It was amusing.

REED: No, if you smile, it's amusing. If you laugh, it's funny.

AUSTIN: I just don't care for double entendre.

REED: What about single entendre?

AUSTIN: Single entendre? Is that a thing?

REED: *(Referring to a woman in the audience)* Yeah. That woman has beautiful breasts. I'd like to touch them.

AUSTIN: What is that?

REED: Double entendre without the double. And speaking of double…

AUSTIN: Stop it! Don't go there!

REED: And speaking of places you shouldn't go, some people think you still shouldn't make jokes about the death of Abraham Lincoln.

AUSTIN: That's true. But to paraphrase the title of Chapter Eight of *The Art of Comedy*, tragedy plus time equals the comic stylings of the inventor of stand-up comedy, President …

AUSTIN/REED: …Abraham Lincoln! Give it up!

(DOM enters dressed as ABRAHAM LINCOLN. *AUSTIN and* REED *greet him and exit.* LINCOLN *uses the microphone to speak, like a contemporary stand-up.)*

DOM/LINCOLN: *(Name of town)*, what's up?! Good looking crowd here tonight, but I gotta tell ya—I'm not crazy about being here. In a theatre.

(If the audience groans)

DOM/LINCOLN: Too soon? Now they call me America's greatest President, and if I am, it's because I am the funniest president. When they accused me of being two-faced I said, "If I were two-faced, would I be wearing this one?" 'Course, it was John Adams who said, "I have come to the conclusion that one useless man is a shame, two is a law firm, and three or more is a congress". And it's still true today. Or Bill Clinton who said, "Being president is like running a cemetery: you've got a lot of people under you and nobody's listening". Or President William Howard Taft, who was so fat—

(He gets audience to say "how fat was he?")

DOM/LINCOLN: President Taft was so fat he got stuck in his bathtub on Inauguration Day and had to be pried out. That shit happened, people! I mean, when President Taft sat around the White House, he sat *around the White House*, you know what I'm sayin'? And George W. Bush said, "My problem with the French is they don't have a word for entrepreneur." And I don't think he was kidding! Now the original stand-up comedians were known as Fools. Every great leader needs a fool, so here are some of the great fools of history:

(He clicks the clicker. A picture of Shakespeare's Fool from King Lear appears.)

DOM/LINCOLN: Shakespeare's Fool from *King Lear*. Yes, fools are jesters and entertainers, but more importantly, they're supposed to tell the truth to power and say things others wouldn't.

(He clicks. A picture of comedian Kathy Griffin appears.)

DOM/LINCOLN: That's right: comedian Kathy Griffin. She can compress the most words into the smallest ideas better than person I ever met. The point is, the best fools make the rest of us look like geniuses. *(This reference can be adjusted to keep it current. You're just looking for someone who talks a lot and doesn't seem to say very much. In the past we've also used "Joe Biden" here.)*

(He clicks. A picture appears of Sean Hannity [or a more recent fool].)

DOM/LINCOLN: Sean Hannity. It is better to be thought a fool than to speak out and remove all doubt. Vladimir Putin is a fool who is dangerous, defiant, and definitely not gay.

(He clicks. A picture of Putin, shirtless on his horse, appears.)

DOM/LINCOLN: And this last fool trumps Putin.

(He clicks. A picture of Trump appears.)

DOM/LINCOLN: That's my time. You been rockin', I been Lincoln. Lincoln out!

(He bows and exits. AUSTIN and REED enter, leading the applause. AUSTIN strikes the mic.)

REED: Abraham Lincoln, everybody! I thought he was hilarious but I saw from the wings that some of you weren't laughing. Maybe you don't know how. That's too bad because studies show the single sexiest trait you can have is a sense of humor. You know what? It's your lucky day. I'm gonna teach you how to laugh. Dom, would come out here?

DOM: *(Entering)* Yeah?

REED: Do you have my clicker?

DOM: *(Handing it to him)* Yeah.

REED: Would you stand over there and help me out?

DOM: Oh, absolutely! I'd love to help. Let me know what I can—

(REED clicks the clicker and DOM freezes.)

REED: Listen. This is how you laugh. When we laugh fifteen facial muscles contract to stimulate the zygomatic muscle of the upper lip.

(REED clicks the clicker. DOM demonstrates what REED describes. It starts out as a smile, but then continues into an exaggerated grimace. It looks painful. REED "pauses" DOM.)

REED: Breathing is interrupted while the mouth opens and closes, making strange sounds.

(REED unpauses DOM. He begins laughing. Then he begins to gasp for air, quietly then very, very loudly. DOM ends up looking much more like he's in pain or having a seizure than he looks like he's laughing. REED clicks to freeze DOM.)

REED: This behavior induces changes in your body that stimulate your organs.

(REED *clicks.* DOM *looks down his trousers and smiles.* REED *clicks again and* DOM *freezes.*)

REED: It increases your heart rate and blood pressure.

(*Click.* DOM *starts stressing out. He checks his pulse at his wrist and neck. He clutches his heart and starts to scream just as* REED *clicks to freeze him.*)

REED: The body then rapidly cools down, resulting in a good and completely relaxed feeling.

(REED *clicks again.* DOM *collapses in a heap.*)

REED: In short, laughter makes you feel good.

(REED *clicks off the lights. Blackout. Lights up on* AUSTIN, *holding a pie and looking at potential targets in the audience.*)

AUSTIN: Hello.

(AUSTIN *looks pointedly at any latecomers and interacts with them as appropriate. Then to the woman who slapped him:*)

AUSTIN: What's your name?

(*He gets an answer.*)

AUSTIN: Really? That's so weird, this pie has your name written on it right here…

(DOM *enters.*)

DOM: Hey Austin, what are you— Woah. Don't! I have a family, man!

AUSTIN: No, Dom, it's all right. I'm just illustrating, again, the rule of threes. The first time you see something it's random. The second time, it's a pattern. The third time is the payoff.

DOM: So you're not actually gonna—

AUSTIN: Not now. This is only the second time we're seeing a pie. Don't worry, Dom. W-W-R-D.

DOM: Why do you insist on saying that?

AUSTIN: Because *The Art of Comedy* is the story of Rambozo. W-W-R-D? What Would Rambozo Do? He would bring the pie.

DOM: Doesn't it concern you that we've finished Chapter Eight and we still don't know how this book ends?

AUSTIN: No, because I have faith. Rambozo is my comedian angel and the theatre is my temple. In fact, this pie illustrates the theatrical principle known as Chekhov's Pie. The great Russian playwright Anton Chekhov wrote that if a pie is shown in the first act, it must be thrown in the second. Chekhov was a comic genius. With all due respect to Plautus and Neil Simon, Chekhov wrote the funniest plays in history.

DOM: No he didn't. Chekhov's depressing. His plays aren't comedies.

AUSTIN: He said they were. They're the original sitcoms. Just like in *Friends*, in Chekhov nobody has a decent job but they all live in amazing homes.

DOM: Yeah. And just like in *Seinfeld*, in a Chekhov play nothing happens. *(He exits.)*

AUSTIN: Exactly! So here now is the funniest Russian sitcom of all time—*Uncle Seagull's Three Cherry Orchards.*

(AUSTIN exits as we hear a famous sitcom theme. DOM/ MASHA enters. All the characters speak with Russian accents.)

DOM/MASHA: Uncle Seagull? Uncle Seagull?

(AUSTIN/UNCLE SEAGULL enters, wearing a bowler hat with two white seagull wings attached.)

AUSTIN/UNCLE SEAGULL: Masha, my dear niece, how you doin'?

DOM/MASHA: Oh, Uncle Seagull, I am so sad. We have wasted our youth and now we have no money. We must sell our three cherry orchards.

(We hear sounds of chain saws chopping down trees.)

AUSTIN/UNCLE SEAGULL: What is that?

DOM/MASHA: Natasha has already begun chopping down the Three Cherry Orchards.

(We hear an explosion outside.)

AUSTIN/UNCLE SEAGULL: And what was that?

DOM/MASHA: *(A la Jimmie J J Walker)* Dyno-mite! The destruction of the cherry orchards represents the way modernization is destroying all that is good in traditional Russia.

AUSTIN/UNCLE SEAGULL: Wouldn't it be more exciting for audience if they actually saw trees being chopped down?

DOM/MASHA: This is Chekhov. All the action happens…

BOTH: …off stage!

(DOM exits as REED enters as NATASHA.)

AUSTIN/UNCLE SEAGULL: *(With disdain, a la Seinfeld)* Hello Natasha.

REED/NATASHA: Hello, Meathead. I have solution to your financial troubles. Sell me your cherry orchards so I can give them to my three sisters—Nina, Pinta and Santa Maria. Bazinga!

AUSTIN/UNCLE SEAGULL: *(a la the Soup Nazi)* No cherry orchards for you!

REED/NATASHA: Hmph!

(REED *exits.* DOM *slides in as* FIRS—*the ancient household servant. He's got a Kramer-like hairdo and mannerisms.*)

AUSTIN/UNCLE SEAGULL: *(A la the gang at Cheers)* Firs! What's up, Firs?

DOM/FIRS: My nipples. It's freezing out there. Sir, I have some bad news. It's Trigorin, sir. He's been shot.

AUSTIN/UNCLE SEAGULL: Where?

(We hear a gunshot offstage.)

BOTH: Offstage.

DOM/FIRS: I'm out! *(He exits in a Kramer-like manner.)*

AUSTIN/UNCLE SEAGULL: Oh, my god! They've killed Triggy!

(REED enters as NINA/Lucille Ball.)

REED/NINA: Waahhh! I got some 'splainin' to do.

AUSTIN/UNCLE SEAGULL: Who killed Triggy?

REED/NINA: It was Natasha! She said she was going to kill you next, Uncle Seagull, if you don't sell her the Three Cherry Orchards.

(DOM runs in wearing the shirt of a Star Trek officer and a bowl cut black wig.)

DOM/CHEKHOV: Captain, Captain! The Enterprise is under attack!

AUSTIN/REED: Wrong Chekhov.

(We hear the ending credits music from a famous sitcom. Blackout. Lights up on AUSTIN.)

AUSTIN: Chapter Nine of *The Art of Comedy*: Show, don't tell. So true. Physical comedy has been around for millennia, but it wasn't until the advent of the motion picture that we could preserve a comedy act in its entirety for future generations. Prior to that, we had to rely on the written word or painted represent—

(DOM *has entered, pulling a rolling bag behind him. He heads for the exit.*)

AUSTIN: Dom! Where are you going?

DOM: To find the missing chapter.

AUSTIN: Where?

DOM: To the Schmulowitz!

AUSTIN: *(Grabbing his bag)* Dom, come back here! You can't leave now in the middle of the show. Besides, we scoured the Shmulovitz. Chapter Thirteen isn't there.

DOM: If we don't have the last chapter we can't finish the show!

AUSTIN: If you *leave*, we can't finish the show! But if you stay and we go as far as we can, we'll at least save twelve-thirteenths of the world! Right?

DOM: Damn your logic!

AUSTIN: Come on, Dom. Nut up. Be bold!

DOM: Okay, then I got this.

AUSTIN: Okay, then I got *this*. *(He wheels Dom's bag off.)*

DOM: Ladies and gentlemen, for this last scene before intermission, we just need to issue a quick warning. We're going to be using a strobe light now, so if any of you are uncomfortable with that—

AUSTIN: *(Re-entering)* Woah, wait— *(Sotto to* DOM*)* I thought we weren't using a strobe.

DOM: Oh, we're using that strobe.

AUSTIN: I thought you reacted badly to strobe lights.

DOM: As a kid, yeah, but I'm totally over it.

AUSTIN: Are you sure?

DOM: Austin—nut up. Be bold.

AUSTIN: *(Exiting)* Okay. Nutting up.

DOM: *(To the audience)* But the strobe may be an issue for some of you and we don't want to have stop the show later. So if anyone's uncomfortable with us using a strobe light, you may seriously leave now. Nobody? Really? Okay— Lights! Camera! Action!

(The strobe light starts. REED enters as Charlie Chaplin. DOM enters as a cop, threatening Chaplin with a billy club. It's quickly clear that the strobe light is making DOM behave strangely. He shakes so much he drops his club and his hat falls off.)

(Standing upright, DOM appears to spin in place without moving his feet. The strobe light's timing matches his movements. Next he seems to glide towards the wings without moving his legs, then he changes direction and glides back on stage. Eventually he collapses unconscious.)

(AUSTIN enters. He and REED and carry DOM's body off. They quickly reenter, carrying a dummy dressed like DOM. They "accidentally" toss the dummy into the wings. Unable to locate DOM, they shrug and exit.)

(DOM staggers back on stage from the wings and falls face down on the floor with arms and legs spread-eagle. He spins in a circle. He "slides" across the stage and back on his knees, then collapses. Again, the timing of the strobe's rhythm makes it appear that he is not using his arms and legs to move. He frantically motions to the booth to turn off the strobe, to no avail. Finally he struggles to the doorway and holds up a sign that says "Intermission". He collapses in a heap as the lights black out.)

END ACT ONE

ACT TWO

(Lights up on AUSTIN *wearing a bowler hat.)*

AUSTIN: Ladeez and gentlemen, boys and girls,
children of all ages! Do you poop out at parties? Strike
out at small talk? Do you feel like the whole world is
laughing but you're not getting the joke? Are your big
yuks just a big yuck? Well, fear not friends! I got puns,
grins, wisecracks, and whizbangs! I got old bits, new
bits, gold bits, and blue bits. I got quick jokes, dick
jokes, and sure to make you sick jokes! I got more boffo
rib-ticklers and one-liner throwaways than you can
shake a shtick at! Where do I keep them all, you ask?
(Holds up a bottle) Right here, friends and neighbors.
You too can learn the secrets of comedy with my very
own surefire one hundred percent guaranteed Elixir
of Laughs! Just one spoonful of my miraculous Elixir
of Laughs will turn a sad sack into a top banana!
What's in it? Why, only the most well-kept secrets of
the Orient and the Borscht Belt, with enough *chutzpah*
for a *shlemiel* or a *shlimazel*, it'll give you *naches* in your
kishkas till you *plotz*! And that's not all, cats and kittens!
We got catch-phrases, spit-takes, double-takes, sight
gags, scene-stealers, show stoppers, snappy patter,
and as a special deal for our Canadian customers, a
poutine routine! That offer's only good in Canada.
Apparently the joke is too. And if you act now, I will
throw in absolutely free of charge a lifetime supply of
dirty limericks, straight from Nantucket! With this—

(As it gets a mild chuckle at best, AUSTIN *repeats the joke for emphasis)*

AUSTIN: I said, straight from Nantucket! With this— *(Dismissing it and moving on)* Fuck it. With this specially blended bottomless bottle of teasers, tag lines, and toppers, you will shock and guffaw the crowd. We got Dead Baby Jokes! How did the dead baby get to the other side of the road? He was stapled to the chicken. Admittedly, these are not for everybody. But if you're an established comic looking to improve his act, or just a beginner who doesn't know the difference between a blackout and blackface, with our extra-strength Elixir of Laughs, you'll be ready for the big time in no time, guaranteed! Side-effects may include uncontrollable milking and painful running gags. For elation lasting longer than four hours, consult your physician. The Elixir of Laughs! If you're not one hundred percent satisfied, well, excuuuuse me!

(Blackout. Lights up on AUSTIN *pulling on a white lab coat.)*

AUSTIN: Thanks very much, ladies and gentlemen. Welcome back. I'm glad to see so many of you stayed. *(This is a good place to make announcements about your next performance or the length of the run or how to connect on social media.)* Now, I know you're probably all wondering whether Dom has recovered from his funny reaction to the strobe. He seems to be okay but just to be safe, I have prescribed bed rest, which I'm actually licensed to do here in *(Your state)* because I once played a doctor on T V. But happily, the title of Chapter Ten of *The Art of Comedy* is "Look Inside One's Self". What a fantastic notion! Can comedy be taught, or is it an inherent quality that you're born with? Since he's already laid up, Dom has graciously agreed to let us peek inside him to see what makes him so amusing.

(REED *rolls on a gurney with* DOM *on it, covered by a sheet except for his head. Like* AUSTIN, REED *wears a white lab coat. It has many pockets for props.*)

AUSTIN: Thanks so much for doing this, Dom.

DOM: No problem.

AUSTIN: Doctor.

REED: Doctor.

AUSTIN: Okay, Dom, let's check your reflexes.

(AUSTIN *taps* DOM *on the knee with a small hammer.* DOM *slugs* AUSTIN *in the belly.*)

AUSTIN: Ow! Good reflexes. You try, Reed.

(AUSTIN *hands* REED *the hammer.* REED *taps the knee closest to him and* DOM *slugs* AUSTIN *again.*)

AUSTIN: Hm. Turn your head and cough.

(REED *turns his head and coughs.*)

AUSTIN: Not you!

(DOM *puts his hands under the blanket and coughs, then:*)

DOM: Aren't you supposed to be doing something while I cough?

AUSTIN: You do it.

DOM: I already am. (*He turns his head and coughs again, then sighs in pleasure.*) You want in on this, handsome?

REED: I'll pass. Should we administer anesthesia?

AUSTIN: Just a local.

(AUSTIN *and* REED *each take flasks out of their pockets.*)

REED: I think that's (*Name of local beer or wine*).

(*They toast and drink.*)

DOM: I think that's my urine sample.

(AUSTIN *and* REED *both do a spit-take.*)

REED: Tastes like Bud Light.

AUSTIN: *(Turning down DOM's blanket)* You seem like you're well on the way to recovery.

DOM: *(Big grin)* I'm feeling better already!

AUSTIN: Okay. Saw.

REED: *(Handing him a saw)* Saw!

DOM: Saw?!

AUSTIN: See? So, here we go.

(AUSTIN saws across DOM's belly six times but the sound effect goes for eight. They looks around to see where the sound effect is coming from. AUSTIN hands it back.)

AUSTIN: Okay, let's look inside and see what makes you so funny.

(AUSTIN pulls DOM's belly incision open and reaches inside. The head of DOM's hospital bed is in an upstage entrance or doorway so that someone can get under the bed and hand props through the incision in the sheets. DOM's head is on a pillow but he is actually standing or sitting underneath the bed frame and sheets.)

DOM: Hey, watch what you're grabbing down there.

AUSTIN: Let's see, what is this— *(He pulls a can of mixed nuts from out of DOM's belly.)* Hm. Dom's nuts. *(He opens it. Snakes pop out ala Snakes in a Can.)*

AUSTIN/REED: Whoah!

DOM: That's what happens when you play with them.

(REED gathers the snakes and puts them into his pockets. For the rest of this scene, after a prop is revealed AUSTIN hands it to REED, who puts it into a coat pocket.)

DOM: I've always enjoyed practical jokes.

AUSTIN: I know you do. Okay, what do we have here? *(Pulling out a large bone)* A large funny bone.

DOM: That's not funny.

AUSTIN: That's 'cause we took it out. Let's see— *(He pulls out Groucho glasses.)* Ooh, Groucho glasses. Classic.

(AUSTIN hands them to REED and pulls out a whoopee cushion.)

AUSTIN: *(Handing it to REED)* A whoopee cushion.

(REED pushes it.)

AUSTIN: Stop that! Wow, Dom. You are all that.

DOM: And a bag of chips.

(AUSTIN pulls out a bag of potato chips.)

AUSTIN: Bet you can't eat just one! *(Pulls out large fake doggy poop; sniffs it)* Ah, Bear claw. *(Or some local delicacy, like Skyline Chili, or Maryland Crab Cakes)*

REED: I hope that's what it is.

DOM: That's what it was.

REED: *(Remembering)* Hey, have you seen—?

(REED exits. AUSTIN pulls out the clicker and clicks it once. DOM falls asleep instantly. He clicks it again and DOM wakes up.)

AUSTIN: Isn't this Reed's clicker?

DOM: *(Taking it, smiling mischievously)* Maybe. How's it look?

AUSTIN: *(Worried, as he pulls out a copy of O magazine)* Ohhh....

DOM: Is it okay?

AUSTIN: *(As he pulls out a copy of OK! magazine)* Yep.

DOM: Am I running out of time?

AUSTIN: *(As he pulls out a copy of Time)* Nope.

DOM: Seriously, how's it going down there?

AUSTIN: *(Struggling with something)* Dammit, Dom, I've got your life in my hands!

DOM: You do???!!!

AUSTIN: *(Pulls a copy of Life Magazine featuring* DOM, AUSTIN *and* REED *on the cover)* Yep, right here. Is it a good issue?

DOM: Delicious!

REED: *(Entering)* Hey, have you seen my notebook?

(A hand holds out REED's *notebook from* DOM's *incision.* REED *takes it and the guys look at the hole, confused.)*

AUSTIN: Wow. What else have you got there?

(The hand reappears squirting a large squirt gun out at the audience.)

DOM: Uh-oh. That's not good.

AUSTIN: C'mon Dom, let's get you sewed up.

*(*AUSTIN *wheels* DOM *offstage.)*

REED: What a cut up. Dominic Conti, everybody! Now, Chapter Eleven of *The Art of Comedy* explains the dynamic of the Double Act thusly. *(Reading from the black spiral notebook)* "In comedy double, Straight Man does set up. Stooge delivers punch line." Straight men were considered more valuable and actually paid more than their comic partners. Then as now in the theater it is almost impossible to find a straight man. So as a tribute to the great comedy duos, here are the Top Ten Funniest Double Acts of all— *(Checking his pockets and finding the clicker missing)* Dom!

DOM: *(Entering)* What?

*(*DOM *sees* REED *holding his hands out. He checks his pockets and finds the clicker.)*

DOM: Wha—? How did that get there?

*(*DOM *hands the clicker to* REED.*)*

REED: *(Dubious)* I wonder. Thank you.

DOM: Believe me, the pleasure was all mine. W-W-R-D! *(He exits.)*

REED: Strange. Anyway, as I was saying, here are the Top Ten Funniest Double Acts of All time.

(He clicks the clicker. A picture comes up.)

REED: Number 10. Penn and Teller.

(Clicks; another picture)

REED: Number 9. Burns and Allen.

(Clicks; another picture)

REED: Number 8. Nichols and May.

(Clicks; another picture)

REED: Number 7. McConnell and Ryan. *(Update this pair as necessary)*

(Clicks; another picture)

REED: Number 6. Key and Peele. Number 5—

(He clicks again. But this time, it's a picture of REED *with a female companion.)*

REED: How'd that get in there? Sorry about that. Number 5—

(Clicks; another picture)

REED: There we go. The Smothers Brothers. Number 4—

(He clicks again. This time it's a picture of two random second graders.)

REED: Oh, this is Johnny DeGlandon who sat next to me in second grade. He could inhale a piece of spaghetti up his nose and pull it out his mouth. And that's the girl who sat next to him and ate it. Number 3—Laurel and Hardy…

(He clicks again. It's a picture of REED *and his female friend in a slightly compromising position.)*

REED: What the...

(He clicks again. It's REED *and his friend again, in even more compromising positions.)*

REED: Dom! Can you come out here?

DOM: Yeah?

REED: *(To* DOM*)* Can you fix this thing?

DOM: Yeah, I can fix this it.

*(*REED *hands* DOM *the remote.* DOM *clicks it, revealing an even more embarrassing photo of* REED *and his companion.* AUSTIN *enters to see what's going on.)*

REED: Stop that!

*(*DOM *and* AUSTIN *think this is hysterical.* REED *now tries to get the clicker back.* DOM *tosses the clicker to* AUSTIN, *who clicks to reveal another compromising photo. He tosses the clicker to* DOM. DOM *fakes* REED *out by pretending to toss the clicker to* AUSTIN, *but keeps it and clicks again. He reveals an image of* REED *in a bubble bath with* AUSTIN. *They are toasting each other with champagne.)*

AUSTIN/REED: Hey!

AUSTIN: That's not funny!

*(*AUSTIN *grabs and clicks the remote as if to turn off the projector. A picture comes up of* AUSTIN *and* REED *in bed with a sheep.* AUSTIN *and* REED *scream.* AUSTIN *clicks the picture off. Blackout)*

(Lights up. AUSTIN *is discovered strumming a ukulele [the chords are shown above each lyric]. He sings.)*

AUSTIN:
C
I laughed till I cried

F
I thought I would die
    C   C7
When Dick Van Dyke came in the door
       F
Tripped over the ottoman onto the floor
C   F
And my very favorite joke machine
              C — A7—Dm—G7
Was *Mad Magazine*
    C
The Knights Who Say "Ni"
      F
They just destroyed me
      C   C7
When Arthur rode across the moors
    F
And Michael Palin said, "One day, lad, all this will be
yours"
(Spoken)
"What, the curtains?" "No, not the curtains, lad.
What's wrong with her? She's beautiful, she's rich,
she's got huge—tracks o' land!"
(Sung)
C   F
Everyone just howled with glee
      C   C7
Not just me
  F
I loved *Looney Tunes*, they were always so funny
Like Porky and Daffy, especially Bugs Bunny
      C   C7
Plus Chaplin and Keaton and Goofy and now Mr Bean
    F
The Coens, the Zuckers, the Farrelly brothers
John Hughes, Billy Wilder and a couple of others

Dm   G7
Made some of the funniest movies that I've ever seen
                     C
They made me laugh till I cry
      F
Plus Laurie and Fry
         C   C7
And the Firesign Theatre and Bob & Ray
      F
Lily Tomlin and Will Farrell and Tina Fey
      C   F
And *Spinal Tap* was my idea of heaven
                  C — A7—Dm—G7
"It goes to eleven"
  C
I laughed till I cried
  F
I thought I would die
         C   C7
Watching 'Make 'em Laugh' in *Singing in the Rain*
   F
Or Woody Allen sneezing cocaine
C   F
Speaking of which, I always loved Richard Pryor
         C   C7
He was on fire
      F
Gilda Radner, Gene Wilder, Bill Murray, Steve Martin
Phyllis Diller and Borge and Mel Brooks & fartin'
         C
Red Skelton, Three Stooges, The Goon Show, and
         C7
Fanny Brice
   F
I loved Danny Kaye in the *Court Jester* sword fight
And *Animal House* with that funny food court fight

Dm   G7
I saw Bill Hicks rant and Second City improvise
      F
And Edmund Blackadder's a bit of a wizard
And Patton Oswalt and Chris Rock, Eddie Izzard
C   C7
And Don Rickles said racist things with a comical snarl
      F
Amy Schumer and Poehler, *The Nutty Professor*
'Weird Al' and Stan Freberg, Tom Lehrer and Frank
Loesser
      Dm   G7
And Groucho and Chico and Harpo and Zeppo and
Karl
      F
The great Peter Sellers—so solemn and silly
And Ricky and Robin and Whoopi and Billy
      C   C7
And Jonathan Winters forever had me on the floor
      F
And Carol Burnett who was funny and generous
Mae West, Dorothy Parker, and Ellen DeGeneres
      Dm   G7
And *Rhoda* and Mary Tyler—and so many more—
*(He seems to consider the many more he could mention…but
decides instead to wrap it up.)*
            C
Anyway, I laughed till I cried
      F
But now I am fried
            C   C7
'Cause things are very tough today
            F
But *Colbert* and *The Simpsons* both make it okay
            Dm   G7
'Cause if I did not know how to laugh—

C—C7—F—C—F9—C

I would cry

(Spoken)

Thank you. Now I'm sorry to say I have some bad news. We've successfully avoided this topic all evening, but the moment has finally arrived. It is time to talk about—*clowns.*

(Blackout)

(Thunder. Lightning. DOM *appears wearing a scary clown mask and wig, holding a flashlight under his chin.)*

DOM: *(Laughing evilly)* Hee-hee-hee-ha-ha-ha!

(More thunder and lightning. The lights switch back to a special on AUSTIN.)

AUSTIN: White-faced demons who haunt our nightmares, baggy-pants enemies of all that is cheerful and good, everyone knows that clowns are floppy-shoed servants of evil. Or are they?

*(*DOM *enters with the spiral notebook.)*

DOM: In Chapter Twelve, *The Art of Comedy* stresses the importance of the clown, saying "No clown, no play", right after the second most important rule, "Don't talk about Clown Club."

AUSTIN: But tantalizingly, Chapter Twelve of *The Art of Comedy* is where we first learn about the life and teachings of the greatest clown of all. A clown of mystery about whom little was known until the man in the black bowler hat revealed *The Art of Comedy* to us.

DOM: Before Bill Irwin—

AUSTIN: Before Emmett Kelley—

DOM: Before the great Grimaldi—

AUSTIN: There was the clown whose name was whispered across the land...

(A recorded voice whispers "Rambozo!" The lights flicker as the word echoes around the theatre. This delights AUSTIN *and worries* DOM.)

AUSTIN: Yes, Rambozo! Chapters One through Eleven hint at his message. But his full glory is revealed in Chapter Twelve, which also predicts that one day Rambozo will return!

DOM: Is he real? No one knows. But the important thing is what he symbolizes—

AUSTIN: Wait a second. Of course he's real.

DOM: We don't know that. Admit it. Rambozo is just a useful cultural myth!

AUSTIN: *(Shocked; aghast)* You don't believe in Rambozo? Have you not accepted Rambozo as your personal joker? Are you an a-humorist?

DOM: I just don't see conclusive evidence—

AUSTIN: You don't see—? Look at history! Who encouraged Christopher Columbus to discover Ohio? You think it's just a coincidence that Lou Gehrig died of Lou Gehrig's Disease? Who calls something a *World* Series and then doesn't invite any other countries? You think that just happens?

DOM: Yes! And can I point out to you that we are now up to Chapter Twelve? And we still don't have Chapter Thirteen, so we don't know how the book ends, so we can't finish the show, so we can't save the world! So I was right! *(Beat)* What? You think these pages are just going to fall from the sky?

(Suddenly, ancient manuscript pages cascade down from the ceiling like autumn leaves.)

DOM: What the—?

AUSTIN: What is all this?

(They gather the pages and look at them.)

DOM: It's in Chinese. What does this say?

AUSTIN: Tsum zao—

DOM: In English!

AUSTIN: *(First reading from one page, then another)* Oh. "Find your inner clown." "Get in. Get the laugh—" *(Realizing)* You know what this is?

DOM: Lemme guess. It's the missing Chapter 13 from *The Art of Comedy*.

AUSTIN: No no no. It's the missing Chapter 13 of *The Art of Comedy*. *(Pointing to a page)* And look! Right here, it speaks of the man named—

(The voice saying "Rambozo!" echoes around the theatre again. They look around.)

DOM: I'm freaking out here!

AUSTIN: No, this is great! Come on, Dom! Think about it: What would Rambozo do?

DOM: I don't know! What *would* Rambozo do?

(Suddenly we hear a gong. REED enters through the center panel as RAMBOZO, wearing a black bowler hat, red nose, and crossed bandoliers filled with bananas instead of bullets.)

REED/RAMBOZO: Get in. Get the laugh. Get out.

(Stunned, DOM and AUSTIN speak together.)

DOM/AUSTIN: You're the man in the black bowler hat!

REED/RAMBOZO: I am.

DOM: You're the man from the Schmulowitz!

REED/RAMBOZO: I am.

AUSTIN: You're the man who revealed to us *The Art of Comedy*!

REED/RAMBOZO: I am.

DOM: You're the man who fluttered these pages down from the ceiling like autumn leaves!

REED/RAMBOZO: I am.

DOM: But you're not actually Rambozo?

REED/RAMBOZO: I am. *(Raises his hand in a grasping claw, ala Darth Vader)* And I find your lack of faith disturbing.

(DOM chokes; letting him go.)

REED/RAMBOZO: Just kidding.

AUSTIN: Dom does not believe.

REED/RAMBOZO: I see all. *(To DOM)* You struggle with your faith.

AUSTIN: I don't!

REED/RAMBOZO: No, you struggle with the ukulele. My good and faithful servants, you have done your best to try to save the world through the message of *The Art of Comedy*. But now you must finish quickly before it is too late.

DOM: Look, Mister Rambozo sir. I'm sorry, but I just don't think the world is that unhappy or dysfunctional a place.

REED/RAMBOZO: Then I don't think you've been paying attention. For instance, let's take a look at my recent experience with those clowns in Washington.

(Blackout. In the darkness we hear a familiar voice.)

NINA TOTIN' BAG: *(V O)* This is National Public Radio Senior Legal Affairs Correspondent Nina Totin' Bag. A series of landmark Supreme Court decisions have left many wondering how the highest court in the land deliberates the issues of the day. N P R has recently uncovered behind-the-scenes footage of the famously secretive body deliberating and it sheds new light on Rambozo's teachings about "puppet governments".

(Lights up on the three guys in black robes. They each hold two Muppety-looking puppets, making them nine black-robed Supreme Court justices. REED *as* RAMBOZO *holds a* CLARENCE THOMAS *puppet on his left hand and a* NEIL GORSUCH *puppet on his right.* AUSTIN *holds a green* ROBERTS *puppet in the center, and* DOM *as* BREYER *is on the left with the* RUTH BADER GINSBURG *puppet on his right hand, held at chest height. Looking at them left to right, the lineup is:* GORSUCH, KAGAN, THOMAS [REED], ROBERTS, ALITO, SOTOMAYOR [AUSTIN], *and* GINSBURG, KENNEDY, *and* BREYER [DOM]. *The puppets have familiar voices.)*

REED/GORSUCH: *(Statler voice)* Order in the court! Order in the court! Let's get back to the question at hand. In a sketch about the Supreme Court, is it allowable to do song parodies of the greatest hits of The Supremes?

AUSTIN/ROBERTS: *(Kermit voice)* Yes! Parody is completely legal and allowable. The court confirmed this in the case of 2 Live Crew.

DOM/KENNEDY: *(Animal voice)* 2 Live Crew! 2 Live Crew! Aaah!

REED/GORSUCH: *(Statler)* 2 Live Crew? Clarence, is that one of those hippity-hop groups? Like Snoopy the Dogg?

*(*THOMAS, *asleep, snores ala Curly Howard.)*

AUSTIN/SOTOMAYOR: *(Swedish Chef; completely incomprehensible)* The court allowed it because 2 Live Crew used *Pretty Woman* to parody pop songs.

(Beat)

DOM/REED: What?! Poop songs?

AUSTIN/ROBERTS: *(Kermit)* No, pop songs.

ALL: Oh…!

AUSTIN/SOTOMAYOR: *(Swedish Chef)* That's what I said. Poop songs.

DOM/GINSBURG: *(Bunsen Honeydew voice)* A parody makes fun of something in the style of the thing it's making fun of.

AUSTIN/ROBERTS: *(Kermit)* Like the songs of "Weird Al" Yankovic. But satire is a different story. Satire ridicules behavior or institutions generally. For instance, *Monty Python's Life of Brian* is a satire of religious fundamentalism.

REED/GORSUCH: *(Statler)* Satire-shmatire! We need to revisit our ruling on gay marriage.

DOM/KENNEDY: *(Animal)* Gay marriage! Gay marriage! Aaah!

DOM/GINSBURG: *(Bunsen Honeydew)* I like big butts and I cannot lie!

DOM/KENNEDY: *(Animal; beginning to hump Ginsburg)* Big butts! Big butts! Aaah!

(Suddenly, music begins and the Supremes break into song.)

REED/GORSUCH: *(Singing)*
Stop! In the name of law
Your words stick in my craw

(But the others gang up on him, with as much choreography as possible.)

AUSTIN/DOM: *(Singing)*
Stop! In the name of law
Your logic has a flaw
Think it oh-oh-ver

(The song shifts to You Can't Hurry Love.*)*

ALL: *(Singing)*
You can't hurry law
No, you'll just have to wait
You know change don't come easy
At least if you're the one to say it (REED *sings "I'm"*)
No, you can't hurry law
And you can't make a fuss
Did you know judicial ethics
Do not even apply to us?
(Spoken) It's true!

(The song shifts to Where Did Our Love Go?*)*

ALL: *(Singing)*
Baby, baby, baby
Where did our laws go?
Ooh, Congress makes them
We just interpret them well
Ooh, Congress, Congress, Congress
Where did our laws go
Thanks to the work we do
Our country's going to hell!

(Big-finish staging. They all bow. Blackout)

(Lights back up on the guys, in their same positions from before the Supreme Court scene.)

REED/RAMBOZO: Now do you see how dysfunctional the world has become because my lessons were lost?

DOM: Kind of.

REED/RAMBOZO: Tell me, what is the title of Chapter Thirteen?

AUSTIN: *(Reading; in Chinese)* Sat yun dik ngai suet.

REED/RAMBOZO: Yes. "The Art of Killing." The vocabulary of both war and comedy is violent. This is why Sun-Tzu was able to copy the final chapter of *The Art of Comedy* word for word and retitle it *The Art of War.*

AUSTIN: So this "missing" chapter actually hasn't been missing for two thousand years.

REED/RAMBOZO: No. In fact, it is the only portion of the book that the world has known.

AUSTIN: But that's good, isn't it?

REED/RAMBOZO: No, out of context its lessons can be painful.

DOM: Come on. To who?

REED/RAMBOZO: Let me show you. Please read Chapter Thirteen of *The Art of Comedy*—

AUSTIN: Which we know as *The Art of War*—

REED/RAMBOZO: Exactly. While I demonstrate.

AUSTIN: *Chuen zin dao*—

REED/RAMBOZO: In English.

AUSTIN: *(Reading)* Sorry. "All warfare is based on deception."

(REED points off stage. DOM looks. REED stomps on his foot.)

DOM: Ow!

AUSTIN: *(Reading)* "Avoid what is strong, and strike at what is weak."

(REED flexes his muscles and gets DOM to do the same, but then REED kicks him in the nuts.)

AUSTIN: *(Reading)* "In war, the secret to success is surprise."

(REED/RAMBOZO takes a rubber frying pan and smashes DOM in the head. There's a loud CLANG sound cue! DOM has had enough.)

DOM: *(Turning on REED)* Slowly I turn, step by step— *(Pointing)* Look, Niagara Falls!

(REED/RAMBOZO *looks;* DOM *stomps on his foot.* REED/RAMBOZO *doubles over, inadvertently tossing the frying pan to* DOM. DOM *catches it, smashes* REED/RAMBOZO *in the face with it, then tosses it to* AUSTIN.)

(*Dom then does a series of Three Stooges moves on* REED/RAMBOZO, *ending with him pulling* REED/RAMBOZO's *arm unnaturally behind his back, then biting his hand. [The arm and hand are both actually* DOM's.])

(DOM *then clicks the clicker, putting* REED/RAMBOZO *to sleep. He holds up a hand mirror and clicks again;* REED/RAMBOZO *sees himself and screams in terror. Frustrated,* REED/RAMBOZO *grabs the mirror and tosses it to* AUSTIN.)

(DOM *grabs his pantomime drill [the one he used in the mime box-building scene], and drills* REED/RAMBOZO's *forehead.*)

(AUSTIN *tosses a slapstick to* DOM, *who tosses it to* REED/RAMBOZO. DOM *spins* REED/RAMBOZO *around by his nipples then purple nurples him, causing him to toss the stick in the air.* DOM *catches it and smashes* REED/RAMBOZO *in the face, then the ass, then the crotch.*)

AUSTIN: Dom, I thought you said you didn't like slapstick.

DOM: I didn't say I wasn't good at it.

(DOM *tosses the slapstick to* AUSTIN *and bows, victorious. We hear a gong as final punctuation.*)

DOM: (*To* REED/RAMBOZO) Are you happy now?

(REED/RAMBOZO *has remained doubled over since the end of the slapstick fight. Now he lifts his head. He's gently laughing.*)

REED/RAMBOZO: Perfectly. In comedy you must give and take. Until you struck back, you were only taking.

DOM: Yeah, because it hurt.

REED/RAMBOZO: Sometimes in physical comedy, there is physical pain.

DOM: Ah! I don't laugh when I'm in pain.

REED/RAMBOZO: Ah! You have mastered the first lesson of Chapter Thirteen. It is not important that you laugh. It's important that *they* laugh.

DOM: *(Realizing)* The needs of the many outweigh the needs of the two.

REED/RAMBOZO: And that is Chapter Thirteen's final lesson.

DOM: Did you learn all these lessons from Ah Tzu?

REED/RAMBOZO: No, he learned them from me. Ah Tzu was my apostle. He wrote down my lessons for the world. But when he was killed the lessons were lost. Now let's go back. What is the title of Chapter Twelve?

(AUSTIN recites it from memory in Chinese.)

AUSTIN: *Sao sok sum ling dik, Rambozo.*

REED/RAMBOZO: Yes. "Find the Rambozo Within." You have searched for Rambozo without. But there's a little Rambozo inside all of us. In you. In me. *(Pointing to* AUSTIN *and someone in the audience)* In you. And in you.

DOM: *(Re: a woman in the audience)* Is there a little Rambozo in her?

REED/RAMBOZO: I'd like there to be. And in order to find your inner Rambozo you must help others find *their* inner Rambozos. Go forth and gather two more apostles. *(To audience, encouraging them to applaud)* Could we get a little encouragement, please?

(REED/RAMBOZO leads the audience in applause as AUSTIN *and* DOM *each bring an audience member on stage.)*

REED/RAMBOZO: *(To them all)* Very good. Thank you for helping us out. Now I need all four of you to raise your right hand and repeat after me. "I, state your name…"

(He waits for them to say that.)

REED/RAMBOZO: "…agree to find the funny…"

(He waits for them again.)

REED/RAMBOZO: "…the whole funny…"

(He waits for them again.)

REED/RAMBOZO: "…and nothing but the funny…"

(He waits for them again.)

REED/RAMBOZO: "…in circus and in health…"

(He waits for them again.)

REED/RAMBOZO: "…So help me, Rambozo."

(He waits for them again.)

REED/RAMBOZO: Okay, I will. You can put your hands down. Every clown must be able to listen and respond. Agree and add on.

DOM: Oh, like improvisation!

REED/RAMBOZO: Exactly. It's called 'Yes, And.' The late Robin Williams was a master at it. So what I'm going to do is teach the four of you how to improvise by having all of you improvise a scene based on suggestions from the audience. Dom, go get two mics. *(To audience volunteers)* What you two are going to do is provide sound effects for a scene that Austin and Dominic will improvise.

(DOM places the mics in front of the volunteers.)

REED/RAMBOZO: Let's have each of you stand behind your own mic. Get real close to it. Whatever happens in the scene, you just make sounds to match. Either of you can make sounds for either Austin or Dom. Speak right into the mics. Don't be shy, just be nice and loud. In fact, let's practice this. Austin, give it a go.

AUSTIN: All right. I'm just going to ring this doorbell here.

(AUSTIN *pantomimes ringing a doorbell. The volunteers make sounds. If they are too shy, try it again. Suggest they may want to say "Ding dong!"*)

REED/RAMBOZO: Dom, now you try.

DOM: Okay, I'm going to honk this car horn.

(He pantomimes that and the volunteers make the sound.)

REED/RAMBOZO: Perfect! Now we're going to need some suggestions for the scene. First of all, we need an interesting location for the scene to take place. *(He takes the first suggestion he hears.)* And now I need the title of a popular, well-known song. What would be the title of a popular well-known song. *(He takes the first suggestion he hears.)* Okay— *[location]* and *[song title].* And you two will provide the sound effects. Off we go!

(They play the Sound Effects improv game, trying to indicate to the audience volunteers lots of obvious places where they can make sounds effects. REED/RAMBOZO can also quietly encourage the audience volunteers to make noises. If the volunteers make lots of noises, then you're golden. If not, lots of laugh can be had by AUSTIN and DOM commenting on the fact that there don't seem to be any sounds, that it's strangely quiet, etc. The whole game lasts 2-3 minutes at which point REED waits for a good laugh from the audience and begins to applaud.)

REED/RAMBOZO: *(To audience)* One more hand for our new improvisers, ladies and gentlemen! Now do you two understand how to improvise?

DOM/AUSTIN: Yes! And!

REED/RAMBOZO: Your final task is to try to become more and more like me each day. Study my life and my teachings so that you too can get in, get the laugh, and get out.

AUSTIN: But we already know your teachings, Rambozo! The great Sigmund Freud tells us—

(REED *takes off his hat and hits* AUSTIN *with it repeatedly.*)

REED/RAMBOZO: No no no! Do not analyze!

DOM: Rambozo, you are so wise.

(REED *hits* DOM *once with his hat.*)

REED/RAMBOZO: Do not suck-up.

DOM: Where did you come from?

REED/RAMBOZO: Backstage.

DOM: I—

REED/RAMBOZO: Go there.

DOM: But—

REED/RAMBOZO: Now.

DOM: *(Exiting and bowing)* Yes, and.

REED/RAMBOZO: Where do I come from? I have always been here. Every culture speaks of me. The Old Testament speaks of an infant found floating down a stream of seltzer water. The Buddha achieved enlightenment when a voice told him "Desire nothing. Serious." To save the world, we need an army of Rambozos.

AUSTIN: But not an army of lame party clowns who only do magic tricks but aren't really funny.

REED/RAMBOZO: Are you kidding? The greatest man in history started out as a lame party clown who wasn't really funny!

(REED *and* AUSTIN *exit.* DOM *enters in a robe and long haired wig looking vaguely Christ-like.*)

DOM: And now for my next trick, I'll change water into wine. (*He pours water from a clear glass pitcher into a glass. It remains clear.*) Oh Me H Christ! This isn't working. Please forgive me.

(REED *enters as* RAMBOZO, *holding a clear glass.*)

REED/RAMBOZO: It seems you are struggling.

DOM: I'm trying, but if I could get this to work, it'd be a miracle.

REED/RAMBOZO: "Do" or "Do not." There is no "try."

(RAMBOZO *pours water from the same pitcher into his glass. The water turns into red wine. [Have dark red Kool-Aid powder in the bottom of this glass when he carries it on.]*)

DOM: Oh my Dad! Thank you, Rambozo! But what will I do next time?

REED/RAMBOZO: Just ask yourself, What Would Rambozo Do?

DOM: What Would Rambozo Do...I'm gonna use that. Wait till I tell the guys. Hey Thomas, you're never gonna believe this—! (*He exits.*)

REED/RAMBOZO: See? The kid turned out all right. He died young, but he did good work. Now undoubtedly some of you are wondering, "Why are other clowns so scary?' Well actually, that was my idea, too.

(*Lightning and thunder. A ventriloquist dummy appears through the seam in the U C panel, with the look and voice of* RICHARD NIXON.)

AUSTIN/NIXON: (*Laughing evilly*) Bwah-ha-ha- ha!

REED/RAMBOZO: Very good, President Nixon.

AUSTIN/NIXON: Please, call me Tricky Dick. Now that you've turned me into a ventriloquist's dummy, people think I'm the personification of evil.

REED/RAMBOZO: That's the idea! It's a trick we teach at the C I A.

AUSTIN/NIXON: The C I A?

REED/RAMBOZO: The Clown Intelligence Agency. Do good work by hiding behind a scary image. You'll be able to create the E P A, endorse Women's Rights—

AUSTIN/NIXON: I'll propose National Health Care! Compared to Republicans fifty years from now, I'll be a pinko liberal!

REED/RAMBOZO: But Mr President, please be careful. I tried ventriloquism once before with Edgar Bergen and Joseph McCarthy. It didn't work out so well.

AUSTIN/NIXON: Don't worry. History will look upon me kindly. I'll designate the first week of August as National Clown Week. It's not funny but it's true. Google it. And as I said on *Rowan and Martin's Laugh-In*, "Sock it to me."

(REED *punches the puppet, who disappears through the seam in the cloth. Loud boxing bell CLANG*)

REED/RAMBOZO: That's right. I taught Nixon to get in, get the laugh, and get out. Of course, we also had Presidents Kennedy and Clinton who got in, got *off*, and got out—but that's a different story. Frankly, I've always been there on the front lines of history. During the American Revolution, when the British were marching in formation in straight lines, I told the Americans not to do what was expected but do what was funny.

(Yankee Doodle *plays.* AUSTIN *runs across the stage in a red coat and powdered wig, chased by* DOM *acting and screaming like an ape. They exit.*)

REED/RAMBOZO: Yes, I invented gorilla warfare.
I invented a lot of things. Funny place names:
Timbuktu. Cucamonga. Lake Titicaca (*Or local place
that is commonly mocked*). But I couldn't always do it by
myself. Sometimes I needed help.

(AUSTIN *runs out dressed as* ALEXANDER GRAHAM BELL.)

AUSTIN/BELL: *(In a ridiculous Scottish accent)* Hoot, mon!
Alexander Graham Bell, reporting for duty, Rambozo.

REED/RAMBOZO: I need you to invent the telephone.

AUSTIN/BELL: Great! What's a telephone?

REED/RAMBOZO: It doesn't matter. I need to make
prank calls. I want to call people and ask if their
refrigerator is running.

AUSTIN/BELL: Sounds like fun! Wait—what's a
refrigerator?

REED/RAMBOZO: Ah, good point. Nikola Tesla!

(AUSTIN *exits as* DOM *runs on as* NIKOLA TESLA.)

REED/RAMBOZO: How are you, Mr Tesla?

(REED *shakes his hand. There's a loud BUZZING sound and
the lights flicker.* DOM *shakes, shocked.*)

DOM/TESLA: What the hell was that?

(REED/RAMBOZO *reveals the joy buzzer on his finger and
hands it to* DOM.)

REED/RAMBOZO: I call it electricity. Invent it, develop
it, give it to George Westinghouse.

DOM/TESLA: *(Exiting)* Got it!

(AUSTIN *pops out as* BELL *again carrying a huge cell phone.*)

AUSTIN: Rambozo, I did it! I invented the first cell
phone! *(Speaking into it and exiting)* Can you hear me
now? Great, can you take me off your calling list now,
ya bastard?

REED/RAMBOZO: And my work continues even to this day, in such places as the Middle East, where my long lost teachings are needed more than anywhere else.

(AUSTIN *enters wearing an Arab head scarf as* DOM *enters wearing the black hat and side curls of an Orthodox Jew.)*

DOM: *(Yelling)* The Land of Israel is a holy place promised to us by God as an eternal inheritance!

AUSTIN: *(Yelling)* You Zionist hoodlums have stolen ancestral land that has been in our family for millennia!

REED/RAMBOZO: Stop it! Stop it! The whole world is sick of this conflict!

AUSTIN/DOM: He started it!

REED/RAMBOZO: Enough! I want each one of you to explain your grievance to me—

(They start talking over each other again)

REED/RAMBOZO: One at a time!

(They start talking over each other yet again)

REED/RAMBOZO: And before either of you say anything else, I want each of you to each breathe in just a little bit a little of this.

(REED/RAMBOZO *hands them each a helium balloon.* AUSTIN *takes the first hit and says in an extremely silly high-pitched voice.)*

AUSTIN: Our hatred is rooted in the deep enmity of our ancestors.

(DOM *takes a hit.)*

DOM: *(In the same high-pitched voice)* You've tried to kill us for millennia.

(They take hits as necessary to continue the conversation.)

AUSTIN: *(Helium voice)* You're killing us now by dividing our nation!

DOM: *(Helium voice)* If you didn't keep trying to kill us, we wouldn't have to!

AUSTIN: *(Helium voice)* Jewish pig!

DOM: *(Helium voice)* Arab dog!

REED/RAMBOZO: Stop! Do you hear yourselves?

AUSTIN/DOM: *(Helium voice)* Yeah—

REED/RAMBOZO: Do you hear how silly you sound?

AUSTIN/DOM: *(Helium voice)* I guess—

REED/RAMBOZO: This is what you sound like to the rest of the world. Now apologize. Use your words. Use your silly voices.

AUSTIN: *(Helium voice)* I'm sorry.

DOM: *(Helium voice)* You should be!

AUSTIN/REED: Hey!

DOM: *(Helium voice)* I mean, I'm sorry too.

REED/RAMBOZO: By the power vested in me, I now pronounce you no longer enemies. In the name of the knock knock, the riddle, and the double entendre.

AUSTIN/DOM: *(Helium voice, like "Amen")* Ha, ha.

(Blackout. Lights up on REED/RAMBOZO *holding the ancient copy of* The Art of Comedy.*)*

REED/RAMBOZO: So that's my life. And these are my teachings. *(Closing the book)* The rest is up to you. Remember that each day is a new chance to make the world a better, funnier place. And now it's time for me to move on.

*(*REED/RAMBOZO *starts to exit.* DOM *runs on.)*

DOM: You can't leave us, Rambozo.

REED/RAMBOZO: I must.

DOM: We're not ready.

REED/RAMBOZO: When you can take the clicker from my hand, you are ready for me to leave.

(REED/RAMBOZO *searches his pockets for the clicker, but doesn't have it. He holds out his palm toward* DOM *who finds the clicker in his own pocket.* DOM *places the clicker on* REED/RAMBOZO'*s palm.* REED/RAMBOZO *gently moves his palm toward* DOM. DOM *easily takes the clicker;* REED/RAMBOZO *doesn't even attempt to close his hand. He shows his empty hand to* DOM *and then to the audience. He points as if to say, "goodbye", and turns to exit.* AUSTIN *runs on.)*

DOM: But we need you!

REED/RAMBOZO: I'll always be here.

AUSTIN: Where?

REED/RAMBOZO: I'll be all around, wherever you look. Wherever there's a fop cracking up a guy, I'll be there. Wherever there's a jester telling truth to power, I'll be there. Whenever a man gets hit in the 'nards, whenever the next "Family Values" politician gets caught having an affair, whenever somebody says, "That's what she said," or whenever somebody calls a bowling alley and asks if they have twelve pound balls, I'll be there. *(Pointing)* Look!

(AUSTIN *and* DOM *look off.* REED/RAMBOZO *quickly exits through the split in the screen. The lights flash and the word "Rambozo" echoes one final time around the theater.)*

AUSTIN: See? I told you. All we needed was a little faith.

DOM: All we needed was Chapter Thirteen. 'Cause now I believe.

(They high-five.)

AUSTIN: Doggone it, Reed missed him again!

(As REED *enters:)*

DOM: He would have loved it.

REED: Loved what?

AUSTIN/DOM: Rambozo was here!

REED: No! Was he talented and good-looking?

AUSTIN/DOM: No!

DOM: He was the guy from the Schmulowitz!

AUSTIN: The man in the black bowler hat.

DOM: He said there's a little Rambozo in all of us. *(Realizing)* I am Rambozo.

AUSTIN: *(Realizing)* I am Rambozo.

REED: *(Knowingly)* I *am* Rambozo.

AUSTIN: *(To the audience)* Say it with us.

ALL: *(Including the audience)* I am Rambozo!

AUSTIN: You too can make the world a better place.

DOM: Don't take yourself seriously.

REED: Bring the funny.

DOM: Fall down more.

REED: Get angry less.

AUSTIN: Tell better jokes.

REED: Question authority.

AUSTIN: Mock the powerful.

DOM: Ridicule hypocrites.

AUSTIN: Fart.

(They each walk to a wing or to the side of the drop, grab a cream pie, and move downstage, pies raised, like they're going to smash someone in the audience.)

REED: And remember: In the the words of the immortal Rambozo, get in—

ALL: —get the laugh. Get—

(REED *and* AUSTIN *smash their own faces with their pies,*
DOM *smashes his crotch. Blackout)*

END OF SHOW

CPSIA information can be obtained
at www.ICGtesting.com
Printed in the USA
FSHW02n1345170518
48362FS